W9-CFQ-457

There, built into the side of the red-yellow cliffs was a hidden village of buildings and towers. Charlie was also amazed by what he saw in the cliffs. "It looks just like a **palace**," he said. The men quickly built a ladder out of long sticks and carefully climbed down to explore.

This is the village that Richard and Charlie saw beneath the cliffs.

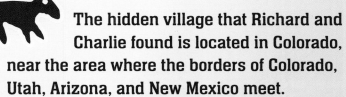

The hidden village that Richard and Charlie found is located in Colorado, near the area where the borders of Colorado, Utah, Arizona, and New Mexico meet.

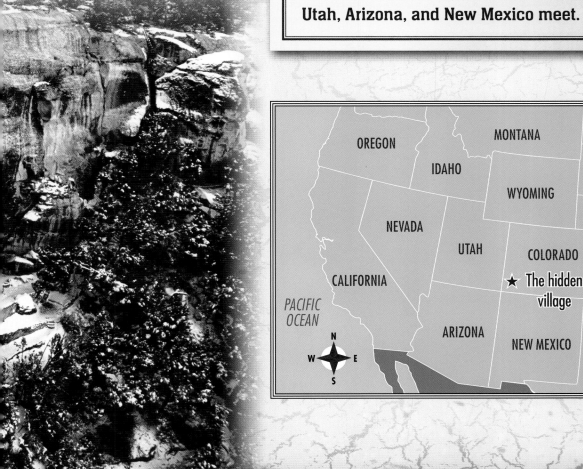

OREGON

MONTANA

NORTH DAKOTA

IDAHO

SOUTH DAKOTA

WYOMING

NEVADA

NEBRASKA

UTAH

COLORADO

KANSAS

CALIFORNIA

★ The hidden village

PACIFIC OCEAN

ARIZONA

NEW MEXICO

TEXAS

N W E S

A Hidden World

Once they were deep inside the cliffs, Richard and Charlie wandered around the village. They went into towers that stretched four **stories** high. Then they uncovered hidden passageways that led to different rooms. Room by room, the cowboys explored a lost world that few people had seen in nearly 600 years.

These are the first buildings in the cliffs that Richard and Charlie explored.

ABANDONED!
Towns Without People

CLIFF DWELLINGS

A Hidden World
CHILDREN'S LIBRARY

by Kevin Blake

Consultant: Ben Duke
Executive Director, Mesa Verde Foundation
Castle Rock, Colorado

BEARPORT
PUBLISHING

New York, New York

Credits:
Cover and Title Page, © CarverMostardi/Alamy; 4, © Nicholas Pitt/Alamy; 6, © Cardaf/Shutterstock; 7L, © George H.H. Huey/Alamy; 7TR, © CarverMostardi/Alamy; 7BR, © George H.H. Huey/Alamy; 8, © AP Photo/Colorado Historical Society; 9, © Kravka/Alamy; 10, © Doug Meek/Shutterstock; 11, © powerofforever/iStockphoto; 12L, © Krzysztof Wiktor/Shutterstock; 12R, © North Wind Picture Archives/Alamy; 13, © Jeffrey M. Frank/Shutterstock; 14, © National Geographic Image Collection/Alamy; 15, © Vladislav Gajic/Shutterstock; 16, © Kravka/Alamy; 17L, © Doug Meek/Shutterstock; 17R, SuziMcGregor/Thinkstock; 18, NPS Photo; 19, © Tony Campbell/Shutterstock; 20, © mark higgins/Shutterstock; 21L, Courtesy of the Library of Congress; 21R, Courtesy of the National Park Service; 22, © George H.H. Huey/Alamy; 23, Courtesy of the Library of Congress; 24, © Lorcel/Shutterstock; 25T, © Ian G Dagnall/Alamy; 25B, Courtesy of the Library of Congress; 26, © Emily Riddell/Alamy; 27, © Kerrick James/Alamy; 28, © George H.H. Huey/Alamy; 29T, © Daniel Lohmer/Shutterstock; 29B, © George H.H. Huey/Alamy.

Publisher: Kenn Goin
Senior Editor: Joyce Tavolacci
Creative Director: Spencer Brinker
Design: The Design Lab
Photo Researcher: Jennifer Zeiger

Library of Congress Cataloging-in-Publication Data

Blake, Kevin, 1978–
  Cliff dwellings: a hidden world / by Kevin Blake; consultant, Ben Duke
      pages cm. — (Abandoned! towns without people)
  Includes bibliographical references and index.
  Audience: Ages 7–12.
  ISBN 978-1-62724-522-7 (library binding)—ISBN 1-62724-522-7 (library binding)
  1. Pueblo Indians—Colorado—Mesa Verde National Park—Antiquities—Juvenile literature. 2. Cliff-dwellings—Colorado—Mesa Verde National Park—Juvenile literature. 3. Mesa Verde National Park (Colo.)—Antiquities—Juvenile literature. I. Duke, Ben. II. Title.
  E99.P9B495 2015
  978.8'27—dc23
                          2014034557

For more information, write to Bearport Publishing Company, Inc., 45 West 21st Street, Suite 3B, New York, New York 10010. Printed in the United States of America.

10 9 8 7 6 5 4 3 2 1

Contents

An Amazing Discovery

On a snowy day in December 1888, two cowboys, Richard Wetherill and his brother-in-law Charlie Mason, stopped at the edge of a deep **canyon** in southwestern Colorado. Richard peered through the falling snow, hoping to find some cattle that had wandered off. Instead, he spotted something strange in the cliffs below. Suddenly, his heart began to race.

Within the rooms, Richard and Charlie found many interesting objects. They discovered children's toys, colorful bowls and jugs, and even a stone ax with leather lacing. Some of their other discoveries were far **eerier**. In one room, they found skeletons scattered on the floor!

Ancient pieces of pottery found inside the cliffs

The area where Richard found the cliff dwellings is called **Mesa** Verde, which means "green table" in Spanish. That's because the area is covered with evergreen trees and is flat like a table.

Digging for Treasure

When night fell, Richard and Charlie gathered the things they had found and went home. Soon, however, they would return to the cliff **dwellings** to continue digging for hidden treasure. For more than four months, they explored the canyon and surrounding area almost every day, finding new **artifacts** and more hidden villages.

Searching for artifacts at the cliff dwellings

At first, the men hoped to become rich by selling the artifacts to museums in big cities. In time, however, the cowboys cared less about making money and became more interested in finding out about their discovery. Who were the mysterious people who had lived in the cliffs? Why did they build villages there? Why did they leave their homes, and where did they go?

Richard and Charlie climbed up and down through the dwellings to explore different levels.

Native Americans had known of the hidden cliff villages but did not enter them. Because people had been buried there, they were considered to be **sacred** places.

The Cliff Dwellers

Different groups of Native Americans had lived in the area surrounding Mesa Verde for thousands of years. Around 550 C.E., a group called the Ancestral Puebloans **settled** on top of the mesa. That's over a thousand years before Richard and Charlie stumbled upon their discovery! The Ancestral Puebloans farmed the mesa's soil and made fine baskets and pottery.

The flat tree-covered area above the cliffs is the mesa. This is where the Ancestral Puebloans first lived.

By the 1200s, after living on top of the mesa for more than 600 years, the Ancestral Puebloans decided to move inside the cliffs. Why? Experts still don't really know. Some think living in the cliffs would have protected the Ancestral Puebloans from **invasions** by other Native American groups. Others believe that living in the cliffs would have offered protection from bad snowstorms in the winter and very hot weather in the summer.

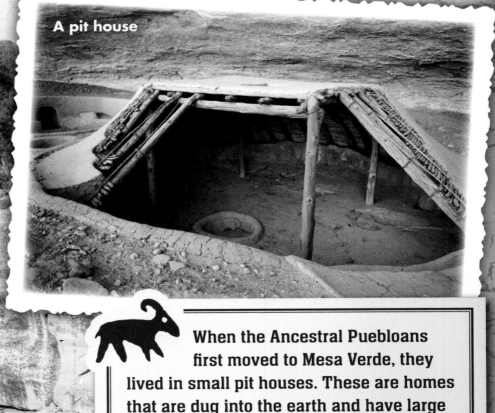

A pit house

When the Ancestral Puebloans first moved to Mesa Verde, they lived in small pit houses. These are homes that are dug into the earth and have large wooden posts that hold up the roof.

Built from Rock

Whatever caused the Ancestral Puebloans to move down into the cliffs must have been very important. Building a home in the side of a cliff takes a huge amount of work—and the Ancestral Puebloans only had simple tools to help them. In addition, everything the builders needed, including food, had to be brought down from the top of the mesa.

Ancient builders had to be careful, especially when they worked near the cliff's edge.

Food and other supplies had to be carried to the cliff dwellings.

To build their dwellings, the Ancestral Puebloans used a soft rock called sandstone. They shaped the sandstone into blocks about the size of a loaf of bread. Then, the Ancestral Puebloans stuck the blocks together with **mortar** made from a mixture of mud and water. Block by block, the Ancestral Puebloans built thousands of structures to form villages.

Experts used the height of the doorways in the dwellings to estimate that the average Ancestral Puebloan man was about 5 feet 4 inches (1.6 m) tall and the average woman was 5 feet 1 inch (1.5 m) tall.

The Ancestral Puebloans constructed large homes block by block.

Life in the Cliffs

More than 5,000 Ancestral Puebloans lived in the cliff dwellings. There, along with dogs kept as pets, the Ancestral Puebloans raised their families. They also died there. More than 212 skeletons have been found in the dwellings—some wrapped in cloth gowns and buried under the buildings.

This picture shows what life might have been like in the cliff dwellings.

While most daily activities took place inside the cliffs, sometimes the Ancestral Puebloans needed to get to the top of the mesa. For example, every morning, people who worked as farmers left the cliff dwellings to tend their **crops**. However, wooden ladders were not long enough to reach the mesa. The Ancestral Puebloans would climb to the top using handholds and footholds carved in the rock— much like modern-day mountain climbers.

Ladders were used to climb short distances up or down.

To move their young children from place to place, Ancestral Puebloan mothers fastened the babies to wooden boards on their backs. The babies spent so much time attached to the boards that the backs of their skulls became flattened.

Cliff Palace

At the center of Ancestral Puebloan life was Cliff Palace, the first and largest village found by Richard and Charlie. Cliff Palace contains 150 rooms and could house more than 100 people. The Ancestral Puebloans probably used the buildings as a place for living and gathering. There were also structures in the village used for **worship**.

Cliff Palace

Some of the rooms in Cliff Palace were painted in bright colors such as red, pink, and yellow. Over time, the colors have faded away.

Cliff Palace has 23 small circular rooms known as **kivas**. These are where the Ancestral Puebloans held religious **ceremonies**. Kivas were often dug into the ground as a way to connect with the earth, which the Ancestral Puebloans worshipped. In kivas, families would also gather to act out stories from the history of the Ancestral Puebloan people.

A ladder was used to enter and exit a kiva. This kiva is located at Cliff Palace.

A kiva

Vanished

It took decades of hard work to build the hidden city. However, by around 1300 C.E., the Ancestral Puebloans had left their spectacular dwellings. The busy cliffs and canyons that were once home to thousands of people were empty and quiet. Why? Experts still aren't sure, but they have two ideas.

For hundreds of years, animals, such as this owl, were the only occupants of the cliff dwellings.

Some experts believe that the Ancestral Puebloans left the cliffs because of a long **drought**. Without enough rain, the Ancestral Puebloans could no longer grow enough food to feed themselves. Other experts think the people moved because of an invasion from a neighboring tribe. They may even have some evidence to support this idea. Some of the skeletons in Mesa Verde are missing their skulls. The invading enemies might have chopped their **victims**' heads off!

A severe drought dries up the soil and kills the plants growing in it.

The Ancestral Puebloans moved to other parts of the Southwest. Several of today's Native American groups, including the Hopi, are their **descendants**.

Getting the Word Out

When the Ancestral Puebloans left their homes, they left many things behind. What remained was protected from bad weather by the cliffs and, as a result, was well **preserved**. That's why Richard and Charlie discovered so many interesting and **intact** artifacts.

Some tools and other objects remain where the Ancestral Puebloans left them, such as these three stone metate (*muh*-TAH-tee), which were used to grind corn.

One reason that the Ancestral Puebloans left things behind may be that they didn't want to carry heavy items, such as pottery and metate, with them.

At first, the cowboys had trouble getting people interested in their amazing discovery. Everything changed, however, when one of Richard's brothers found a small **mummy** of a child in the ruins. Newspapers ran stories of the cowboys' amazing find. The stories interested a young Swedish explorer named Gustaf Nordenskiöld who had been living in the United States. In 1891, the Wetherills showed him around the ancient cliff dwellings. Gustaf's mouth dropped open in amazement.

This colorized picture of Cliff Palace was taken in the 1890s, soon after the cliff dwellings began to gain national attention.

Gustaf Nordenskiöld

Stop That Man!

From morning to night, Gustaf taught the Wetherills how to dig without ruining the artifacts. He showed them how to use small **trowels** rather than big shovels that could break fragile objects. Gustaf labeled and photographed everything, hoping to make a complete study of the Ancestral Puebloans. He also had another plan: to send everything he found back to museums in his home country of Sweden!

Today, scientists continue the careful research begun by the Wetherills and Gustaf.

After spending two months with the Wetherills, Gustaf left Mesa Verde with boxes of Ancestral Puebloan artifacts. When he reached the nearest railroad station, a local sheriff arrested him for trying to remove the objects from the United States. It turned out, however, there was no law protecting the precious **antiquities**—so Gustaf took everything he had with him.

Gustaf left Colorado with many artifacts aboard a steam-powered train.

Gustaf saved everything he could find in the dwellings, including ash from fire pits, trash, and even human waste that might reveal what the Ancestral Puebloans ate.

Protecting the Past

After Gustaf ran off with Ancestral Puebloan artifacts, some Americans decided it was time to take action and protect what was left. One woman, Virginia McClurg, worked hard to save the cliff dwellings from treasure hunters. Fortunately, she was a famous writer of that time. She wrote many newspaper articles suggesting that the Mesa Verde area should become a **national park**.

In 1872, Yellowstone became the first national park in the United States.

Virginia also formed the all-women's Colorado Cliff Dwellings Association to ask Congress to make it a crime for people to remove artifacts from the site. In 1906, she succeeded in her goals. President Theodore Roosevelt signed a law making Mesa Verde a national park. It was the first park to protect things made by people.

The entrance to Mesa Verde National Park

President Theodore Roosevelt helped protect more than 230,000 acres (93,077 hectares) of American land, including Mesa Verde National Park.

Mesa Verde Today

Because of the work of **preservationists** such as Virginia McClurg and President Roosevelt, more than 500,000 people now visit the cliff dwellings each year. The Mesa Verde National Park covers 52,000 acres (21,044 hectares) in southwestern Colorado. Visitors can hike and climb up ladders the same way the Ancestral Puebloans did a thousand years ago.

Mesa Verde National Park is a very popular tourist attraction.

When the Wetherill family first dug in the cliffs, one younger brother said that he could feel the eyes of the Ancestral Puebloans watching him. Every day, new visitors come to explore the buildings and can wonder whether the mysterious cliff dwellers are still watching them.

The cliff dwellings at night

In 1978, the cliff dwellings were named a World Heritage Site by the United Nations because of their importance to human history. The Egyptian pyramids and the Great Wall of China are also World Heritage Sites.

Mesa Verde: Then and Now

THEN: Thousands of Ancestral Puebloans lived in the cliffs of Mesa Verde in sandstone homes around 1200 C.E.

NOW: No one lives in the cliffs of Mesa Verde. Only birds, lizards, snakes, and other animals make their homes there.

THEN: The Ancestral Puebloans used stone tools and axes to build their homes.

NOW: People use power tools and large machines to build homes.

THEN: The average Ancestral Puebloan person lived to be about 33 years old.

NOW: The average American lives to be about 78 years old.

THEN: The average Ancestral Puebloan man was 5 feet 4 inches (1.6 m) tall.

NOW: The average modern-day man is 5 feet 9 inches (1.7 m) tall.

If you are tall, make sure to duck when entering the doorway of an Ancestral Puebloan home.

THEN: Pottery and tools were used in Mesa Verde by the Ancestral Puebloans.

NOW: Pottery, tools, and other objects taken by Gustaf Nordenskiöld can be seen at the National Museum of Finland.

THEN: Ancestral Puebloan farmers would climb the side of the mesa to reach their crops.

NOW: Thousands of tourists climb up and down ladders to see where the Ancestral Puebloan farmers lived.

GLOSSARY

antiquities (an-TIK-wi-tees) objects from a long time ago

artifacts (ART-uh-fakts) objects of historical interest that were made by people

canyon (KAN-yuhn) a steep-walled valley carved out by a river

ceremonies (SER-uh-*moh*-neez) events that mark a special or sacred occasion

crops (KROPS) plants that are grown and gathered for food

descendants (dih-SEN-duhnts) people who come from particular ancestors

drought (DROUT) a long period of time with little or no rain

dwellings (DWEL-ings) places where people live; homes

eerier (IHR-ee-uhr) more mysterious, stranger

intact (in-TAKT) not broken or harmed

invasions (in-VAY-zhuhnz) events where a group enters by force or takes over, usually in a harmful way

kivas (KEE-vuhz) round ceremonial rooms built into the ground

mesa (MAY-suh) a hill or mountain with steep sides and a flat top

mortar (MOR-tur) a mixture of sand and water that is spread between bricks or stones to hold them together

mummy (MUHM-ee) a dead body that has been preserved

national park (NASH-uh-nuhl PARK) an area of land set aside by the government to protect everything that is found there

Native Americans (NAY-tiv uh-MER-uh-kinz) the first people to live in America

palace (PAL-iss) a large, grand place to live

preservationists (*prez*-er-VAY-shuh-nists) people who try to keep land, nature, and historical objects safe

preserved (pri-ZURVD) kept in good condition

sacred (SAY-krid) holy, religious

settled (SET-uhld) made a home and lived in a new place

stories (STOR-eez) floors or levels of a building

trowels (TROU-uhls) small modern tools with curved blades used by archaeologists to dig holes

victims (VIK-tuhmz) people who are hurt or killed by other people

worship (WUR-ship) a show of love and devotion, usually of a religious nature

BIBLIOGRAPHY

Arnold, Caroline. *The Ancient Cliff Dwellers of Mesa Verde*. Boston: Houghton Mifflin Harcourt (2000).

Fitzgerald, Michael. "The Majesty of Mesa Verde." *The Wall Street Journal* (March 14, 2009).

Sanchez, Robert. "Ghosts on the Mesa." 5280: *The Denver Magazine* (March 2012).

READ MORE

Aveni, Anthony. *Cities Buried Beneath Us: Discovering the Ancient Cities of the Americas*. New York: Roaring Brook Press (2013).

Collins, Terry. *The Mesa Verde Cliff Dwellers: An Isabel Soto Archaeology Adventure (Graphic Expeditions)*. Mankato, MN: Capstone (2010).

Croy, Anita. *Ancient Pueblo: Archeology Unlocks the Secrets of America's Past*. New York: National Geographic (2007).

LEARN MORE ONLINE

To learn more about the cliff dwellings at Mesa Verde, visit
www.bearportpublishing.com/Abandoned

INDEX

ABOUT THE AUTHOR

Kevin Blake lives in Portland, Oregon—not a ghost town!—with his wife, Melissa, and son, Sam. This is his fourth book for children.